BRITAIN IN OLD PHOTOGRAPHS

CHESHAM

YESTERDAY & TODAY

COLIN J. SEABRIGHT

SUTTON PUBLISHING

Sutton Publishing Limited
Phoenix Mill · Thrupp · Stroud
Gloucestershire · GL5 2BU

First published 1996

Copyright © Colin J. Seabright, 1996

Cover photographs:
front: The old market hall, 1895
back: Part of the High Street, 1903

British Library Cataloguing in Publication Data
A catalogue record for this book is available from the
British Library.

ISBN 0-7509-1267-7

Typeset in 10/12 Perpetua.
Typesetting and origination by
Sutton Publishing Limited.
Printed in Great Britain by
Ebenezer Baylis, Worcester.

The Park and Avenue pictured in 1905 from Dungrove Hill looking across the roof-tops of Broadway.

CONTENTS

A typical Chesham scene, with industry among the houses, this 1915 photograph shows the timber yard at Beechwood Brush works, behind the houses of Sunnyside Road.

INTRODUCTION

There is evidence of occupation in the Chess Valley from the Stone Age to the Romans, but the first recorded reference to Chesham is in 970 in the will of Lady Elgiva. She was the wife of King Edwy, who had been responsible for diverting the river to power the original Lord's Mill, creating Chesham Moor in the process. Entries in the Domesday Survey of 1086 record four mills in the town and imply a thriving local iron industry. The parish church was built in the twelfth century and added to in the fourteenth and fifteenth centuries. It underwent major alterations in the eighteenth century including construction of the spire and installation of the clock, and was largely restored in 1869. Nonconformity has always had a stronghold in Chesham where the first Baptist church was established in the seventeenth century. By the end of Victoria's reign there were four Baptist, one Congregational and two Methodist chapels, and one Quaker meeting house, together with a Salvation Army citadel.

The market was established in 1257 and Chesham became the focus for the surrounding countryside and neighbouring villages. Chesham's prosperity in the Middle Ages was due to the market and mills and to its craftsmen, who made shoes, gloves and breeches from locally cured leather. They were joined by a small-scale clothing industry employing weavers, dyers and tailors, and a local mill was converted for fulling cloth. Later craft industries, based on locally grown materials, included straw-plaiting, chair-bodging and general wood-turning, and these, together with lace-making, occupied the townsfolk until the eighteenth century.

In the nineteenth century work became more industrialized, with the first small factories producing boots, brushes and all kinds of woodware, but specializing in domestic and dairy utensils and shovels (later in toy buckets and spades, and hoops, for which there was a great demand). Growing businesses needed new factories, which were built outside the limited confines of the original town. This area was known as Newtown, immediately to the north up the narrow valley. Here a mixture of industrial and residential properties allowed most of the artisans to work within a stone's throw of their own front doors.

Waterside, a separate community at the other end of the town, grew in the same way, accommodating new factories and sawmills between the existing houses. Here also were cottage industries based on the River Chess, growing watercress and breeding ducks, a popular Victorian delicacy.

At the beginning of Victoria's reign, the commercial heart of Chesham was Church Street, while the High Street was mainly residential, including at least half of those classified in directories as gentry. Gradually the emphasis changed, with traders taking over both Market Place and High Street. By 1894, when the Urban District Council was set up, Chesham possessed all the services and amenities of an up-to-date Victorian town, including a railway link to London which brought increased prosperity to all its businesses and industry.

The balanced industrial and residential mix kept local people in the town for work, resulting in a strong community spirit, and for many, even in the early twentieth century, to venture as far as Amersham was a rare occurrence, and longer journeys were not even contemplated, despite the railway.

Subsequent growth and changes are illustrated in this volume, in which pictures from yesterday (from about 1880 to 1950) are compared with the same scene today. The pace of change has increased in recent years, mostly in the interest of traffic, or of commercial greed, but it is left to the reader to judge whether or not these changes are also in the true interest of Chesham and its people.

Those familiar with Chesham will find that parts of their town are not pictured here; this is because those fortunate areas have managed to remain virtually untouched by 'progress' and the scenes today are very similar to the earliest available views.

The old Red Lion Inn, Market Square, 1900.

WATERSIDE

Waterside, a separate community some half a mile downstream from the town centre, but very much a part of Chesham, developed alongside the River Chess and the stream diverted a thousand years ago to provide the power for Lord's Mill. Although the mill has been demolished, the 2 acre millpond is still a major feature of the area. Part of Waterside was officially within Chesham Bois parish until the boundaries were revised in 1934, hence the title of the illustration below.

This 1895 view of the newly built houses along Bois Moor Road also shows watercress beds in a former gravel pit to the right of the view. The viewpoint is now within the Cresswell Road estate, and buildings completely hide any view today.

The marshy ground of the Lower Moor alongside Bois Moor Road suffered from gravel extraction during construction of the railway. It is pictured here in about 1915 after flood waters from heavy rainfall in the upper Chess Valley expanded the normal gravel lakes to cover a very wide area.

The Lower Moor was drained, filled (using the town's domestic refuse) and levelled in the twenties and thirties. The resultant open field, between the River Chess and the mill stream, was used as a sports ground.

Slightly up river, the stream below Lord's Mill carried a considerable flow of water in 1920. There was a slope into the water from the road beside the flint cottages, where horses could enter to cool off or quench their thirst. This also served as a bypass, avoiding the busy corner in front of the mill, by fording the stream to another slope facing the mill.

Today there is much less water in a rubbish-strewn river bed, and modern flats behind the trees have replaced the old cottages.

The same stretch of water, looking back towards Lord's Mill, is pictured here in 1928, when the seventeenth-century mill was still busy grinding grist and animal feeding stuffs. The other slope of the ford can be seen between the cottages and the bridge.

The mill ceased operation in the fifties, was allowed to decay, and was finally demolished in the eighties despite considerable local pressure to preserve it.

This 1895 view is across the millpond's overflow stream to the Waterside Ironworks next to Lord's Mill. Here Sidney Cheeld & Co., mechanical engineers and specialist artesian well borers, later manufactured the 'Easy Churn' and other dairy utensils, and also built motor cars.

Today the old building still houses an engineering works, but the thatched cart-shed in the centre disappeared when the old cottages were replaced, in 1933, by Norjo-An Villas.

Despite the caption, this is not the river, but a view along the millpond, pictured in 1905 with Aylesbury ducks on the bank. They would have belonged to the duck-breeders living in the cottages on the other bank.

Riverside Court was built on the site of the cottages and sheds in 1964, and today's ducks are wild, but well fed. The trees on the bank were planted in 1926 to beautify the scene, but those in the water are self-sown in the silt of the slow-moving water.

The Island stood between two branches of the Chess, reached by a narrow footbridge from Moor Road. Pictured in 1910, the house was screened by trees from its industrial neighbours – Bois Steam Saw Mills (a typical Chesham turnery and woodware factory), and the Canada Works (which made portable poultry houses).

The old house still stands, though turned into offices, and since the early eighties it has shared the island with a very modern industrial building, necessitating a wide concrete bridge for vehicles.

Waterside is the name of the main road as well as the local community, and in this 1930 view Rose's Stores, a butcher's and grocer's since 1805, stands across the road from some very old cottages, a small garage, and the Elephant & Castle public house.

Several cottages on the left made way for a massive expansion of the garage; those in the centre of yesterday's view were replaced by a factory, situated in front of the gasworks. Rose's Stores finally closed in 1977.

Pictured in about 1950 this sixty-year-old girder bridge carried the railway line over the main road and adjacent factory yard at Waterside. The steam-hauled train is about to start the long climb out of the valley to Chalfont & Latimer.

Today's scene includes new rolling-stock, introduced in 1960, crossing the 1986 replacement bridge. Initially the cost of replacing the worn-out bridge threatened the continuation of Chesham's rail service, but luckily London Transport managed to find sufficient funds.

Chesham, and Waterside in particular, became famous for its watercress, of exceptional quality owing to the iron-rich waters of the River Chess. The cress-beds on this 1900 postcard were in the heart of the community, with the backyards of cottages in Waterside on the other side of the flint wall.

Today the area has been concreted over and is used as a car park for the adjacent engineering works. The last remnants of the flint wall are the only recognizable feature from the Victorian era.

SECTION TWO

THE AMERSHAM ROAD

From the foot of the Amersham hill, the road leads past Mineral Cottage, the site of a nineteenth-century attempt to establish a spa based on the mineral-rich waters of an adjacent spring. It then takes you via Red Lion Street, once known as London Road, into Market Square.

Amersham Road leads into Red Lion Street at the junction with Waterside. This 1945 view includes the ornamental gardens laid out on the site of the Pound after it was purchased for road-widening in 1937. The public open space has since been extended as far as Meades Water Gardens over former watercress beds reclaimed in 1979. Mature trees restrict today's view from the same point.

Although the direct Amersham Road had been constructed in 1820 to replace the old turnpike round the side of the hill, the title 'New Road' was still in common use in 1895. Here, at the foot of the slope, it passed Amy Mill. The mill had closed down about ten years earlier when the owner, George Rose, transferred all milling operations to Lord's Mill, but the house remained.

In the seventies Amy Mill House was demolished to make way for a traffic roundabout, and the remainder of the site has recently been tidied up as 'Friedrichsdorf Corner', named after Chesham's German twin town.

During the short-lived attempt to promote Chesham as a spa, the waters had been dispensed from Mineral Cottage, just off the road behind the trees. Its ornamental gardens, to the right of this 1900 view, had, by then, been converted into more watercress beds.

Since 1947 a garage has occupied the filled-in site of the cress-beds, and now, without the tree screen, the old cottage can be seen to the left of the garage forecourt.

In 1895 the old Punch Bowl Inn, seen here, stood at the corner of the cobbled Punchbowl Lane, with its entrance in Red Lion Street. Next door up the lane was the old Baptist chapel of 1719, and across the lane, facing the side of the inn, The Forelands, a large house of similar age.

The new Hinton Baptist chapel was built on the corner site in 1897. The Forelands still stands, now the Baptist manse – its walled grounds are used for garden parties and fêtes.

In this 1900 view along Red Lion Street, the Nags Head, owned by the Amersham Brewery, advertises their brew, 'Wellers Entire', on its prominent chimney. At this date a weekly sheep market was still being held in the yard, in front of the inn's stables.

In the twenties the yard and stables became the Nags Head garage, then in the thirties the whole site was cleared for road-widening, and a postwar office development now occupies the surplus land.

This 1900 view from Market Square shows the narrow end of Red Lion Street, a tight squeeze even for light horse-drawn vehicles; the first hint of the problems likely to come with heavier traffic at this bottleneck on the main road to Amersham and the capital. As early as the late twenties, the council was considering road-widening, but this required using the powers of compulsory purchase. The necessary local act was passed in 1930 for major widening, which extended well into Amersham Road. All buildings on the west side of Red Lion Street were demolished, starting in 1937, and the new Red Lion was built round behind the old, opening just before the war.

The urgent need for improvements is even more evident in this 1932 view of an Amersham & District bus negotiating Red Lion Corner.

Now the road is both wider and straighter; these improvements are beneficial for today's increased traffic, much of which has no business in Chesham, but simply uses the Amersham–Chesham road as a short cut between motorways.

From the end of Red Lion Street, Townfield Yard, a collection of cottages, workshops, a boot factory, another Baptist chapel and the White Lion Inn. This community climbed the side of the valley, continuing as steps to the railway footbridge and path to Dungrove. This 1930 view is back down the Yard from the steps.

All was swept away under a 1932 Slum Clearance Order and replaced by a community of old people's residences, part of which is seen in today's view.

MARKET SQUARE

Market Square, at the southern end of the High Street, is believed to have been laid out in the thirteenth century. The original market hall was rebuilt by Lord Chesham in 1856. Later managed by a business consortium, it housed a general market on the open ground floor, while the upstairs hall was used for both entertainments and official purposes, including the magistrates' court. The market hall was demolished in 1965 to improve traffic flow, but the square has subsequently been pedestrianized and the original clock from the hall reinstated in a modern tower on its site.

On 5 August 1919, Market Square was the venue for Chesham's peace celebrations, when crowds gathered in front of the hall to witness the dedication of a temporary war memorial consisting of a simple wooden cross.

This 1895 photograph shows Market Square before complete commercialization gave rise to major rebuilding on the east, right-hand, side. At this time several of the properties were still residential and the post office occupied the premises on the right with the porch. Here Miss Agnes Maria Devereux presided over an office which opened from 7 a.m. to 8 p.m. on weekdays and for three hours on Sunday mornings for the full range of postal services including telegraph business and savings bank transactions. The adjacent gateway gave access to the sorting office from which there were three delivery rounds on weekdays and one on Sundays. The last posting times were 7.45 p.m. for London and the North, carried by rail from Berkhamsted, and 4.45 a.m. for same day delivery to local destinations. In the building on the other side of the passageway, George and Arthur Smith, who were later to publish a very wide selection of local view postcards, had recently moved their stationery shop from nearby Church Street.

A 1939 postcard view from the same point shows Market Square as many residents will remember it with affection. After the reconstruction at the turn of the century, subsequent changes were limited to shop-front alterations.

Following the demolition of the Market Hall, the square remained an open space, initially carrying all the town's through traffic. Since the 1968 opening of St Mary's Way, which necessitated some demolition on the west side, this traffic now bypasses the square.

Looking in more detail at the east side of Market Square, this 1900 view, after the recently completed face-lift, shows the Oak Tree Boot and Shoe Company's shop in a new building where Smith Brothers and the post office yard had been. Smiths had moved into the former post office, with a proper shop-front added to an otherwise unaltered building. Beyond them Herbert's grocery stores had been rebuilt with a gabled roof over a modern frontage, and further modernization had been carried out on the neighbouring premises towards the High Street. The following four views have all been taken from very nearly the same spot, and together they illustrate the minor, but steady, progress and changes made to a small corner of the shopping centre.

This 1912 postcard shows little structural change to the square, but far more traffic than at the start of the century. It also gives a good view of Smith Brothers' shop window with over 150 postcards on display, mostly from their own range of at least 200 different views of Chesham and local villages.

By 1928 motor vehicles were becoming far more common and in this view an open truck is making a delivery to 'Chesham's only walk-around Drapery and Clothing Store', situated under the arches.

In 1950, before the postwar boom in car ownership, the occasional horse-cart was still to be seen on the streets of Chesham. The market hall then housed Kerr Brothers' textile trimmings factory.

Today the square is more open since the demolition of its central building, replaced in 1992 with a tower of locally made bricks supporting the restored, original clock, which had been housed in a council depot for the previous twenty-seven years. All very attractive, but a poor substitute for the old hall!

The Oak Tree Boot and Shoe Company was a subsidiary of Reynolds, a well-established firm in the traditional local industry, listed in directories from 1877 as 'James & Edwin Reynolds, wholesale boot & shoe manufacturers, curriers & leather merchants, contractors to the British & foreign governments'. Pictured here in 1903, their shop offered a wide range of footwear, including heavy boots at 4s 11d a pair and ladies' lightweight shoes from as little as 1s 9d.

After many changes of trade, the front of the shop is unrecognizable today.

This photograph, taken on Coronation morning, 1911, shows Thomas Whiteman's stores, well decorated for the occasion. Beside the shop was the entrance to Lewin's Yard, named after Robert Lewin, a mid-nineteenth-century 'grocer, provision merchant, tallow chandler and cheesemonger' in Market Square.

At the start of the First World War, Florence Whiteman took over from her husband. Then, in 1923, they were bought out by Kingham's – the shop remained a branch of their high-class grocery empire until about 1960.

Looking the other way in 1907, with a horse-drawn carriage outside No. 17, which still appeared more like a house than business premises, despite the fuel order notices over the door and window.

Since 1935 No. 17 has been occupied by Brazil's, with the typical tiled window of a traditional butcher's shop.

Turning now to the west side of the square, this 1895 view shows Gomm's butcher's shop, with open windows above a marble counter, a shop-front which remained unchanged until the building was demolished in 1968. Yet another butcher opened in the premises next door at the turn of the century, just out of the picture, and suffered the same fate.

St Mary's Way now runs where the two butcher's shops used to stand.

Pictured in 1913, when Frederick Ralph Hutton was the proprietor, the Chequers Hotel offered teas and 'Good Accommodation for Cyclists'. A tied house of Weller's Amersham brewery, it was partially hidden from view behind the market hall.

The Hotel closed after the Second World War and became the headquarters of the Chesham Building Society. Pictured here in August 1995, the building was decorated following the 150th birthday celebrations of what is now the oldest building society in the world.

An uncommon view of the market hall, seen here from the end of the High Street. This photograph was taken in 1905 when the Union of London and Smiths Bank temporarily occupied part of the ground floor while awaiting completion of their new permanent premises further along High Street. The lamp over the hall's central arch announces 'Fire Station', where the horse-drawn pump was housed until the early twenties.

The arches of the new tower were designed to reproduce the style of the old building, and the clock is nearly, but not exactly, in its old position.

THE OLD TOWN

The historic parish church stands on a slight eminence to one side of the main valley, and Church Street, the medieval heart of old Chesham, still contains many ancient cottages gathered closely in the shadow of the church. The main commercial street until the latter part of the nineteenth century, it only gradually lost this role to Market Square, High Street and the Broadway. Neighbouring Germain Street also contains many old houses, but lacks the obvious charm which pervades the whole of Church Street. Immediately behind the church, the extensive grounds of the park, reaching to within a few yards of the shopping centre, were given to the town in 1953 by the Lowndes family. The most outstanding feature of the park was a magnificent avenue of seventy-six elm trees, leading from the churchyard gates.

The church stands proudly above the roof-tops of Church Street in this 1900 view, looking over the market hall from the Dungrove path, above Townfield and the railway line.

Germain Street starts from a corner of Market Square and soon crosses the infant River Chess at Town Bridge. The picturesquely named Duck Alley, a community of thirteen terraced cottages, photographed here in 1920, faced the stream below the bridge.

The original cottages were removed under a Slum Clearance Order in the mid-thirties and a new printing works for the *Bucks Examiner* was built in their place. This in turn has given way to redevelopment, currently taking place on the site.

Pictured in 1932, this view of Town Bridge is one of dozens of similar postcards of probably the most photographed Chesham scene. The foreground slope gave vehicular access to Water Lane, a track along the riverbed to the nearby mill.

The corner shop just over the bridge also disappeared with the rest of Duck Alley, and the wide approach to Town Bridge has long been used as an unofficial free car park, with vehicles often almost in the water.

Looking along Water Lane in 1935, tree trunks for William Wright's Steam Saw Mill are piled up on the far slope out of the water. Behind the fence and trees, the open water-meadow extends to the back of How's brewery and the houses, shops and boot factories in Church Street.

The sawmill and brewery buildings were demolished in the sixties and the site grassed over as a public open space.

One of the most attractive views of the church was obtained from the edge of the water-meadow near Town Bridge, pictured here in about 1900.

Today, although the old buildings below the church are unchanged, the foreground is considerably less attractive, since the water-meadow was drained and surfaced as a public car park.

Germain Street continues as Fullers Hill, a hedge-lined lane between open fields, pictured here in 1920. At its first bend a gateway gave access to a popular footpath across the Cow Meadows to Beech Wood and Chesham Bois.

Today the road still runs out into open farmland, but since the fifties the Fullers Close housing estate has stood across the old footpath, its entry point where the gate used to stand.

Missenden Road, the outward continuation of Church Street, also runs through open country immediately beyond these Lowndes Estate workers' cottages, which were empty, and about to be rebuilt, when photographed in 1919.

The replacement terrace, described by Pevsner as, 'picturesquely grouped around a courtyard in the garden suburb idiom', still marks the end of the town in this direction.

This 1930 photograph of Church Street includes some of Chesham's oldest buildings, a line of sixteenth-century timber-framed cottages with oversailing upper floors. The furthest of these, the Old Sun, was originally a pilgrims' inn or guest house for visitors to the nearby parish church.

This end of the street suffered major changes in the late thirties – the oldest cottages were demolished, but the Old Sun was re-erected as a private house at Pednor. Official buildings of a temporary nature have occupied the site ever since.

Pictured in 1905, Barnes coach-builders had been in business since 1848, initially as wheelwrights. Keeping up with the times, their 1907 directory entry added 'Motor bodies painted and trimmed'.

Barnes' premises and their immediate neighbours were demolished in the fifties, the site remaining empty for over ten years until construction of the first phase of St Mary's Way routed traffic across it and along the edge of the park.

Behind the church, the Avenue, pictured here in 1914, led across the slope of the park to the foot of Chartridge Lane. It was the only north-south route apart from the High Street, and had to serve as a traffic bypass whenever the latter was closed for any reason.

Now, sadly without the majestic line of trees, and without grazing sheep, the Avenue runs between formal flower beds and closely mown grass.

Staying in the park, this is how the lake looked in about 1900. Townsfolk had almost unlimited access to the Lowndes family's private grounds, but had to share the space with the resident cattle from Catlings Farm, the buildings of which can be seen between the trees. At this date the park presented a wild, informal look, with a natural muddy bank to the lake, which included a very poor, unkempt specimen of an island.

Pictured again in 1935, the park had undergone major improvements in the mid-twenties, when leased from the Lowndes family as a public recreation area. The lake was edged with concrete and deepened sufficiently to allow boating around a new island, and steps from the lakeside led to a paved, circular rose garden and on to the Avenue.

Later changes included a fountain in the circle with a cascade down to the lake. The island was renovated in 1996 to provide safer nesting places for the resident waterfowl.

This 1895 photograph shows the buildings of Catlings Farm in the upper part of the park. Although the Avenue runs along the lower edge of the farm, the line of trees never extended past the farm buildings. The Broadway can be seen over the farm, with the Congregational chapel prominent in the centre.

Since 1902 the most prominent feature of the Broadway has been the domed turret of the General Baptist chapel, now accompanied by several other tall, but less distinguished modern buildings. Nothing remains of Catlings Farm and its site has long been grassed over.

Returning to Church Street, we now come to the part which has suffered most in recent years. The bottom end of the street is seen here from the Market Square corner in 1890, when most of the buildings were still in commercial use. On the left, another carcase is being delivered to Caroline Payne's butcher's shop to add to those already hanging in the window. Beyond this an unbroken line of small shops includes a fishmonger, a greengrocer and two bakers; the last shop visible on this side being the original Darvell's bakery, then still run by Sarah, the widow of George Darvell, who founded the firm in 1838.

A slightly wider view from almost the same spot in 1935, when most of the shopkeepers had moved to the High Street and the premises had reverted to private houses. The only business remaining were two boot repairers, with Reeve's 'Working Mens Tea Rooms' on the other side just along from the Golden Ball.

The first few houses on the right were demolished in 1937 and the next block by 1950; then in 1968 the first stage of St Mary's Way swept through the open site, its second stage later resulting in wholesale demolition of the other side of the road.

Another of William Butts' photographs of the bottom end of Church Street, this 1911 view includes Reeve's pawnbrokers and army surplus stores, and the partly hidden front of the Golden Ball, where publican Harry Wing was also the local knacker and unofficial vet.

The remnants of Church Street can be seen today, past a new office block on the site of the Golden Ball's stables. The inn closed, but escaped demolition and is now used as a doctors' surgery.

HIGH STREET

Mainly residential until well into the nineteenth century, the High Street then gradually took over as Chesham's commercial centre, and during the second half of Victoria's reign some cottages gained shop frontages and others were rebuilt as shops. This change was hastened by the opening of the railway station, just off High Street where it leads into Broadway. An interesting feature of Chesham's High Street was the number of small residential yards entered by archways between the shops. These were mostly named after previous owners of those premises and gave attractive open views of the Park on one side, or Dungrove Hill on the other.

Pictured by William Butts in about 1895 at the beginning of High Street looking back into Market Square, a group of workers is here employed on some major works. The large steam pump, outside the premises of dentist Edward Mawer, suggests that deep excavation is involved, probably in connection with the sewers. The bay-windowed building, then apparently unoccupied, appears little altered today, now housing 'The Tiger's Eye'.

The entrance to High Street from Market Square, pictured in 1899 with an interested group of onlookers of all ages.

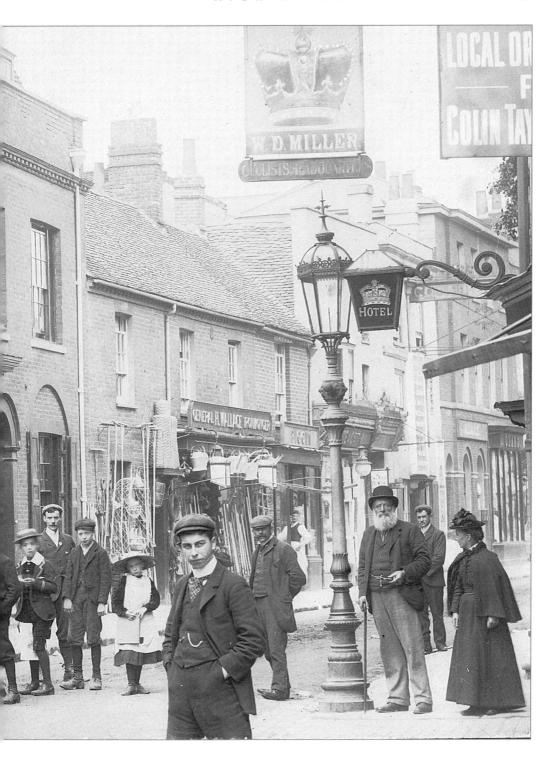

The same view today, in which many of the old buildings are still recognizable above their modern shop-fronts.

In 1911 the photographer still drew an uninvited audience! This slightly faded view shows more of the right side of the street, including the front of the Crown Hotel. The first building on the left had been remodelled at the beginning of the century, with its previous sharp corner cut away at an angle.

This 1950 view shows few structural changes in forty years, but the Crown has had a slight rearrangement of its doors and windows, and the archway which used to give access to the 'livery & bait stables' now leads to 'Victoria Hall Restaurant and Saloon Bar'.

The historic Crown Hotel was demolished in about 1960 and a supermarket built on the site. The striped blind at the edge of the view is over Brazil's butcher's shop, next door in Market Square.

This general view of the shops in High Street was published in 1910. The Queen Anne-style building on the right is the impressive new branch of the Union of London and Smiths Bank, recently occupied following their temporary sojourn in the market hall. Next door to the bank at No. 11 is the crowded window display of Patterson's drapery which had followed the trend and moved here from Church Street in 1903. Facing them is another of Chesham's historic inns, the George and Dragon, a seventeenth-century timber-framed building which had been re-fronted in about 1715.

In 1935 the most noticeable change is in the traffic, with many cars parked outside the shops and businesses, particularly the bank, now the National Provincial and Union Bank of England. Pattersons had expanded into No. 9, and the Midland Bank had recently moved in next door to their rivals, while, just beyond the banks, Chiltern Wireless Stores had been 'authorized agents for Pye and Marconi' for over ten years.

Today the large bank is simply NatWest, and since Pattersons closed in 1982, their spacious showrooms have been divided into separate shops again.

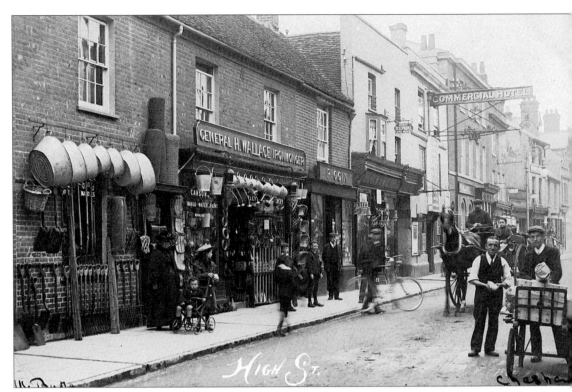

This animated 1900 photograph gives a more detailed look at the west side of the street. The display of ironmongery from Wallace's, who first opened here in 1890, extended not only over their own frontage, but also that of the private house next door. Their other neighbour was the new grocer's shop of George Piggin, a family business which was to remain until after the Second World War. Humphrey Blower was landlord of the George and Dragon, even then usually abbreviated to the George, where the yard housed the Parcel & Enquiry Office of the L&NWR, and the front still displayed a huge notice, the full height of the first floor, announcing 'parcels accepted here for carriage by London and North Western Railway to all parts of the UK'. Carriage by road to their nearest station at Berkhamsted had offered the only nation-wide goods service before the Metropolitan Railway opened their direct rail service from Chesham.

A closer look at the George in 1906, still bearing its railway notice. Next door beyond the inn, the many-talented Daniel Clare was not only a linen draper, but also secretary to the Gas Light & Coke Company, local representative for Gilbey's wines and spirits, and agent for the Alliance and Crown Insurance Companies.

A listed building today, the George and Dragon is unaltered, even retaining the original sash windows. Its immediate neighbour has only a new shop-front, but most of the other buildings have suffered major changes.

Looking back towards Market Square, this 1915 view includes, on the extreme left, another of Chesham's long-lived businesses, where, in 1900, the Cox family had taken over the saddlery established by William Lacey in 1845.

Today Cox's shop has a modern frontage, but the old building can still be recognized.

Worlds Stores opened their Chesham branch in 1905, at 25 High Street, separated from the saddlery by Lacey's Yard. In this picture, the manager and staff of the stores posed outside their premises in 1925, shortly before they moved to Market Square.

25 High Street today is a seventies replacement building, but Lacey's Yard remains.

This particular part of the High Street is adjacent to photographer Butts' studio and shop, and a large picture of Chesham church can be seen in his window at the edge of this 1903 view. The landlord of the Stag doubled as greengrocer within the same building and the chemist next door advertised his second calling with a large pair of spectacle frames over the window.

The Stag has now been replaced by modern shops, but the other buildings are only superficially altered.

Edwin and Walter East occupied Butts' former premises from about 1924, selling stationery, books, newspapers, and their own sepia postcards of local views photographed by Walter. On their shop, in this 1930 view, they announce their agency for Goss porcelain figures, a wide range of small pots and models bearing the town or county crest.

East's remained in business here until after the Second World War, and the building is hardly changed today.

This Butts view of High Street, where it opens out into Broadway, dates from about 1885, and, as with other nineteenth-century pictures, the presence of the photographer with his heavy wooden tripod and other paraphernalia has attracted a good crowd of onlookers. At this date, the railway was still only in the planning stage, and Station Road, which was soon to interrupt the line of dwellings, was not even thought of.

Pictured from approximately the same spot in 1910, almost all the buildings had been replaced in the previous twenty-five years. Station Road now enters on the right, the junction flanked by an impressive building for the Bucks and Oxon Union, later Lloyds, Bank on one side, and Henry Parker's Chess Vale Temperance Hotel on the other.

Today's view shows the later changes, with a typical late twenties building at the far end, and equally typical seventies monstrosities on the left.

This photograph shows a 1907 procession headed by the town band, under the banner of 'St Mary's Church Chesham Sunday and National Schools' marching along High Street into the Broadway. The tallest building was then still a private dwelling, and next door beyond it was a 'ladies' boarding school' run by Mrs Elizabeth Darvell and Miss Emily Maude.

The only original buildings remaining today are those either side of the former school. The school itself was rebuilt, as Woolworths, in the thirties and all those to the left were replaced in the late sixties.

THE RAILWAY

T he opening of the Metropolitan Railway into Chesham in 1889 gave a welcome boost to local trade and industry. It brought cheaper fuels and made the delivery of outgoing products quicker and easier, particularly advantageous for perishable goods such as the Aylesbury ducklings for the London meat markets. But it was only because of the persistence of local people that the railway had reached Chesham town at all, as the economy-minded railway company at one time proposed to reduce engineering works by terminating the line on the Moor, although later plans suggested an extension over the hills to Tring, via Chesham Vale. After a long descent from Chalfont Road to the valley at Waterside, the line climbs the last half mile through cuttings on the edge of Dungrove Hill to the station and on into the goods yard.

In this 1890 view from the front of White Hill school over the station yard, deeply excavated from the hillside, one engine shunts past a two-coach train standing at the station platform, while another stands beside the cattle dock on the road leading to the goods shed.

Goods Station, Chesham.

Viewed from White Hill looking towards the station in about 1910, the goods yard was a hive of activity, with a wide variety of goods on assorted wagons occupying all four sidings. The facilities had already been increased to meet the immediate demands of freight traffic, which continued to grow steadily to a peak in the mid-twenties when the yard was handling some 50,000 tons per annum. A considerable proportion of this was coal, brought in for domestic and industrial consumption and especially for the town's gas and electricity works until local production and generation ceased. Many other raw materials arrived for the town's factories, including a fair amount of imported timber to augment local supplies. The cattle pens handled livestock both arriving for and departing from the district's farms. Much of the output of Chesham's traditional industries was carried by rail, including consignments of boots and shoes, brushes and other woodware, also watercress in sufficient quantities to require its own special evening train for Covent Garden market.

After the 1967 closure of freight operations, the levelled ground was turned into a large car park. The station remains and its distinctive platform canopy can still be seen in the distance.

Pictured in about 1888, this view during excavation work on the line outside the station, somewhere above Townfield, gives an idea of the depth of chalk removed to achieve the required track level.

In 1888 the goods shed is still under construction, with smartly dressed men working on the unfinished roof. Behind the building, the skyline trees are in the upper park at the far side of the valley.

After a long and very busy life, the goods shed was demolished in 1968. A new road between the supermarket and the car park is now routed across its site.

A 1959 picture shows the station just prior to electrification. It gives a view into the yard where the main tracks to the goods shed were aligned for the proposed Tring extension along the side of the Chesham Valley.

Today, with a restricted view past the buffer stop, the obsolete but well-maintained signal box supports a multitude of hanging flower baskets, part of the display which won first prize in the railway station gardens competition in 1996, a regular event for the station's green-fingered staff.

In another picture from the year before the railway opened, an engine and truck well loaded with officials passes out of the yard into the station site.

The end of the remaining track has been enclosed by a brick wall and only the coal stands remain as a reminder of the busy goods yard. Beyond them, a concrete wall hides the original, sheer chalk face.

Viewed from the footbridge carrying Elm Tree Hill footpath over the line in about 1945, this rolling stock, three of the oldest Metropolitan Railway carriages of 1898 vintage hauled by an ex-Great Central Railway locomotive, survived in daily service on the line until electrification in 1960.

Today's train, of graffiti-covered A60 rolling stock, is pictured on the same track. Owing to the anti-vandal 'cages' surrounding all footbridges it is no longer possible to photograph the line from the centre of the bridge.

Access to the new station necessitated the construction of Station Road, and this is what it looked like for the first few years. It was photographed in 1894, looking down towards Broadway.

The Bucks & Oxon Union Bank opened in 1898 on the High Street corner of Station Road, with the Chess Vale Temperance Hotel upstairs over Catling's millinery shop on the opposite corner. Since then the buildings have remained the same, apart from the construction of East Street in about 1970.

BROADWAY

Broadway, a widening of High Street at its junction with Blucher Street, was originally known as Pillory Green, the site of the town stocks and lock-up until 1833. Also the traditional venue for the charter fairs, and all kinds of both unofficial and ceremonial gatherings, it was still used for this purpose until the Second World War. As with the rest of High Street, the transition from residential to commercial use took place in Victoria's reign, and the northern continuation of High Street followed the same trend, but somewhat later, with a few private houses remaining into the thirties. Blucher Street, leading past the Park to Chartridge Lane, remained mainly residential until its final demolition in the 1960s.

In June 1921 crowds gathered in Broadway for the unveiling of Chesham's war memorial, a magnificent statue of a soldier 'at ease' which had been purchased by public subscription.

This 1897 photograph clearly shows the extent of the Broadway, then an uninterrupted open space between the main part of High Street and its northern continuation, sometimes distinguished as Upper High Street, in the centre of the view. At the right edge of the picture, William Ivory's coffee house heads a group of busy shops, with an assortment of goods and plenty of customers lining the pavement.

This 1930 postcard was photographed from the same point. The small island around the war memorial was then regarded as the town's bus station, where an early Dennis bus of the Amersham & District Bus Company prepares to leave for the Amersham terminus at the Griffin Hotel.

Today traffic islands and partial pedestrianization break up Broadway's original open space.

Now our first view of the west side of Broadway, photographed in early morning sunshine during 1900.

Looking at the same group of buildings from the other direction in 1910, the most striking feature is the decorated plasterwork covering the front of the Lamb, a mid-Victorian addition, which increased the town's total of drinking places to seventy (for a population of just over 7,000). In the decades since the previous view, the post office had moved away to its permanent premises at the beginning of Upper High Street, and the Easts had opened their first shop. Next door to the pub, Markham's ironmongery shop had been taken over by Brown's, who were destined to remain in business there for nearly seventy years.

These two present-day views are taken from the same viewpoints as those on the facing and previous pages. The left-hand shops gave way to a particularly ugly, concrete supermarket development in the late sixties, and slightly less obtrusive stores replaced the Lamb and its neighbours in the early seventies.

Turning now towards Blucher Street, this 1903 view includes the new Broadway Baptist church. Next, beyond the church, the Star public house marks the start of Blucher Street. The building on the right, towering above the neighbouring cottages, is Brandon's furniture shop.

In the late twenties Brandon's opened smart new showrooms in place of the old cottages. The Star was demolished in 1938, as was the remainder of Blucher Street during the sixties, which opened up views to the park.

Pictured in 1895, the General Baptist chapel, or Star meeting house, was built at the edge of Broadway in 1712. Beside it, behind the lamp post, was the entrance to Star Yard, a community of fourteen small cottages between the Star and the edge of the park lake.

Growing congregations required a larger building and the 1902 replacement Broadway chapel, of red brick and cream stone, completely filled the site.

Taken from outside the park gates looking towards Broadway, this 1925 view of Blucher Street shows its terrace of seventeenth-century houses stretching from the Blue Ball to the Star, and the facing cottages with their well-cultivated gardens.

All was swept away in the sixties during the construction of St Mary's Way, and a traffic roundabout now occupies the site. The only remaining Blucher Street building is the timber-framed structure opposite the Baptist chapel.

A 1907 photo from outside the Cock gives the general view of Broadway looking south. Prominent in the centre is John Tree's drapery, which projected in front of the general building line. The wide street gave plenty of room for horse-drawn vehicles with complete safety.

A 1955 view from exactly the same spot shows remarkably little change in fifty years. The wide street was then well used for parking, with cars three or four abreast outside the Lamb. (Courtesy of the Francis Frith Collection.)

Today's view shows the destruction wrought by developers in the last forty years, with uninteresting, standard commercial buildings in place of the attractive mixture of old and individual façades, which characterized the real Chesham.

A closer look at the east side in 1915 shows the International Stores in the large premises on Station Road corner, now with the Chesham Club and Literary Institute upstairs. A few doors along, the frontage of the newly opened Chesham Palace cinema included shops on both sides of the entrance.

The corner building is unaltered apart from its shop-front, and the upstairs now houses a nightclub. The next three have been completely rebuilt but bay windows on one try to re-create the style of its predecessor.

Pictured here in 1940, the Palace has become the Astoria, modernized in 1930. Behind the flagpole, Cameo House, with its decorative frontage, dates from the post-railway rebuild of 1890, and the war memorial soldier has stared across the traffic since 1921.

Since the 1959 closure of the cinema, various retail businesses have occupied the site, but little else has changed apart from the additional obelisks and roll of honour beside the war memorial and the shape of the island containing it.

This photograph, showing the old Congregational chapel, was taken in about 1880, shortly before the small, simple 1724 building was replaced. The large residence to the left then contained a butcher's shop at its far end.

The 1886 chapel, with its decorative turrets like rockets ready for the launch, now serves the United Reformed church. The old house became the main post office from 1903, but was recently converted into a new pub and shop.

An 1885, pre-railway, view of the very rustic looking north side of Broadway, including the entrance to Upper High Street. Although some of the occupants of the cottages sell local produce from their front parlours, there are no signs of commercialization, and a small hanging painting of a cockerel is the only indication of the Cock Tavern. In the roadway at the centre of the view a solid, ornate plinth supports a single gas lamp.

A 1900 postcard view from the same point, but looking slightly further to the right, shows the rebuilt Cock Tavern boldly advertising Salter's Ales, an import from outside the county. The tall building to the right of the previous photo is the only identifiable feature remaining, at the centre of this view.

The subject of today's picture is a wider angle view, which is taken from the same place but covers both the previous scenes. It can still be identified by the same building standing on the corner of Upper High Street, but virtually everything else has changed again.

This part of the High Street was, in 1910, still partly residential, but also contained the premises of some of the more uncommon traders, including manufacturers of braces and belts, of artificial teeth, and of umbrellas, as well as a cabinet-maker and a sewing machine shop.

Most of the right-hand side has been rebuilt twice since the previous view, firstly between the wars, including a large departmental store for the local Co-Op, and again in the last decade for modern shops.

Yesterday's view of the end of Upper High Street, in 1907, shows the recently rebuilt Waggon and Horses, another inn advertising Salter's 'Splendid Ales', despite its location almost facing the Chesham Brewery at the foot of White Hill. Next door, beyond Waggon Yard, the 6½d Bazaar is almost hidden by a horse-drawn carriage waiting at the pub, and another carriage stands outside Foster's cycle shop a few

Pictured in 1890, a group of locals gathered outside the original Waggon and Horses, where a strange advertisement on the frontage is for Winkley & Shaw, 'Horse Slaughterers, by Appointment to Her Majesty'. The old building was replaced by the present inn at the turn of the century.

The Victorian building remains unchanged today, but a 1970 supermarket development has replaced most of its old neighbours.

BROAD STREET & NEWTOWN

B y about 1880 factories and houses occupied all the available land on the floor of the valley as far as Townsend Road. Further expansion created Newtown, a similar mixture of homes and workplaces up the valley, north of this unofficial boundary, and also spread residential development up the surrounding hillsides. By the end of the century development extended a full mile from the town centre, or two miles from the far end of Waterside, making Chesham one of the longest towns in the country for its overall area.

Fire was an ever-present hazard in the lightly built woodware factories, and this was the aftermath of a serious blaze at Jesse Wright's sawmill in Berkhamsted Road on 3 May 1907. The fire caused £5,000 worth of damage to the workshop and machinery, and destroyed the outhouses of neighbouring cottages.

White Hill, or Hempstead Road, the old road to Codmore and Botley, climbs steeply up the side of Dungrove Hill from the end of High Street. This 1910 view, back down from the first sharp bend, shows the road squeezing between the main brewery buildings on the left and its stables on the right.

Modern developments of offices, shops and flats now occupy the brewery sites, and White Hill has been both widened and straightened, giving a clearer view of the Waggon and Horses at the bottom.

Above the corner of White Hill a tree-lined hollow, known as Martyr's Dell, is believed to be the site of Thomas Harding's martyrdom in 1532. In this wintery scene of about 1890, part of the dell is being used as East's timber-yard, with a weatherboarded storage building.

After the closure of the timber-yard, trees and scrub gradually filled the hollow, but houses now occupy the site, screened by the remaining trees.

In 1903, Alfred Walker was landlord of the Three Tuns Inn on the very edge of the bend in White Hill, where it created a dangerously blind corner on the steep hill. A solid Victorian building, its neighbours up the hill were equally solid, terraced Victorian villas. After compulsory purchase for road-widening in 1963, the inn saw temporary service as council offices before its final demolition.

This 1890 photograph is of the original Three Tuns Inn, housed in a cottage on the same site until just before the end of the century.

Since the demolition of the Victorian building in the sixties, the site has been turfed over, the resultant open space allowing clear views round the corner for the safety of traffic negotiating the hill.

Soon after entering Broad Street we come to the Chesham citadel of the Salvation Army, pictured in 1906 when it was decorated for the forty-first anniversary of the Army's foundation by William Booth. On one side is William Dear's general store, while the plot on the other side remains empty.

A small, detached house was built next door to the citadel in the sixties and the old shop has been given a very modern frontage, but the Salvation Army building approaches its centenary exhibiting very little change.

Until 1880 Townsend Road really did mark the end of the town. Pictured here in 1905, looking towards Bellingdon Road, its typical Chesham mix of houses and works included Robert Webb and Sons' brush works; one of the first real factories in this well-established local craft, situated across the road from East's woodware factory.

The Victorian houses remain today, but a do-it-yourself store and a warehouse complex stand on the sites of the brush works and woodware works respectively.

Pictured in 1885 the continuation of Broad Street still resembled a country lane even though it contained the 1861 police station, and had the benefit of street lighting. Since about 1870 gas from the Waterside works of the Chesham Gas & Coke Company had illuminated all the town's main streets.

Two years after the previous picture, the terrace of Cestreham Villas was built on the field next to the police station, and by 1910 the road was well developed with houses on both sides.

The old police station was demolished in 1931, and its impressive replacement, incorporating a courtroom, is pictured here the following year. Next door, behind the tree, was the Wesleyan chapel.

The police have recently moved to a new, smaller station on the site of the chapel, and their previous building has been converted into an office block, now named Copsham House.

Pictured in 1885, this broad section, which gave Broad Street its name, was created where a pair of cottages had once stood in the middle of the roadway.

Just into this century, and from a slightly different viewpoint, new villas occupy the right-hand field, and a pair of houses with 'look-out' windows on the second floor have been slotted in on the left.

Infilling is now complete, but today's view is otherwise mainly the same except for some new shop-fronts and the war-time loss of iron railings from garden walls.

Higham Road lies at the heart of Newtown. Pictured in 1885, with East's woodware works in the background, this thatched cottage, originally the water bailiff's house, is only a few yards from Broad Street beside the stream from the Higham Mead springs. It pre-dates the main development in the road.

Despite the Victorian and Edwardian development just along the road, the cottage remained for many years, but a sixties warehouse development, which replaced the woodware works, also covered the cottage site.

The main development of Higham Road started further along the road, beyond the old cottage. Pictured in 1910, the road then contained two boot factories and four brush works. Behind the right-hand houses Chesham Electric Light & Power Company's generating station had supplied power to the town since 1904.

Today's scene is remarkably similar, although most of the works now produce very different goods. However, George Tutill & Company are still making flags and banners here, as they have since 1920 – in the extreme right-hand premises.

Broadlands was the Victorian mansion set in extensive grounds high on the hillside. In this 1905 view it is seen from the bottom of Eskdale Road between the Jolly Sportsman and the old cottages at the end of Broad Street.

After the First World War, Eskdale Road was extended as Eskdale Avenue, and the old cottages at its foot were replaced by a new block, including, for the next fifty years, a baker's shop. Broadlands Avenue was developed on the site of the big house in 1958.

At the turn of the century, Eskdale Road was built-up as far as the first bend and petered out a hundred yards further on. By 1915 the extension up the hill had been started, but was without houses when this view was taken from the middle part of the road, looking across the fields of Taylor's Farm and the roof-tops of Cameron Road and Alexander Street. The main Berkhamsted Road, with its terraced villas, runs the length of the valley across the middle of the picture, and a short line of houses up the far hillside marks the start of Addison Road, with Alma Road further to the left. By 1930 Eskdale Avenue was well established all the way up to the junction with White Hill, and the next view includes several of the large houses in the middle section of the road. The far hilltop was then well covered by the council development of Pond Park estate, started two years earlier to house those displaced by slum clearance schemes in the town centre.

This 1930 view from the same point is through a convenient gap in the line of housing development.

Today there is still a gap between the houses at the same place, but a very mature hedge completely obscures the view there. This picture was taken from behind a neighbouring block of flats and therefore has a different foreground.

Sunnyside Road was the northern limit of Newtown until about 1900. Pictured in 1912, this part of it was mainly residential, with half a dozen small shops among the houses. Behind the left-hand houses were the factories of Higham Road, see page 4, while the cemetery limited development on the other side.

Today, apart from the traffic, there is little visible change, but most of the shops have closed. The cemetery still forms an oasis of peace and quiet between Sunnyside Road and later developments on the hill, further north.

Pictured in 1905 the New Inn was 237 Berkhamsted Road, where James Jackson was licensed 'to sell by retail Beer Porter Cider & Perry to be consumed on the premises'. It dates from the early 1880s, when it served the first residents of Alexander Street and George Street and the workers of the neighbouring boot factories and sawmills.

In about 1960 the inn was demolished and Alexander Street widened as part of a scheme which replaced many of the old, terraced houses by blocks of flats.

This 1900 view is of one of the still undeveloped sections of Berkhamsted Road, looking over the grassy space opposite the council's waterworks to the first houses of Brockhurst Road. In the middle, the houses of Eskdale Road stand well above the roof-tops of Alexander Street.

The site remained open until construction of Newtown Baptist church in 1927 and the infant school a few years later. In today's view the school building is screened by fully-grown trees in its grounds.

A better view of the new buildings is given by this 1932 view looking the other way, when the trees were only saplings.

This 1930 view of the residential edge of Newtown is from the upper slopes of Nashleigh Hill recreation ground, looking along the chimneys of Severalls Avenue snaking away into the distance, with Brockhurst Avenue to the right and the first few houses in the dip below Nalders Wood on the left.

The most striking difference in today's view is the number and size of the trees – not only in the recreation ground, but also in any vacant spaces between the houses.

Sporadic development started beyond Berkhamsted Road into the Vale just before 1900, and the Nashleigh Arms was one of the first buildings. Pictured in 1905, when landlord George Gibson offered 'Weekend Accommodation' for the many visitors who came from London to enjoy the Chiltern countryside, the inn then faced the first of a line of houses recently built on Handpost Meadow, but the corner plot remained vacant. Vale Road suffered badly from flooding after any heavy rains further up the valley, and this picture shows the aftermath of a flood with pools of water and a layer of debris remaining in the road.

By 1930 development was complete well into Vale Road and on the corner of Nashleigh Hill across from the inn, and was beginning on the other hillside below Pond Park.

Today, development extends to the edge of the historic Vale Farm, and a garage stands on the corner opposite the inn, its name now officially reduced to the abbreviated form commonly used, the Nash Arms.

The Vale Farm, Chesham

Pictured in 1900, Vale Farm then stood remote from the town along Chesham Vale, which was the road to Cholesbury and Tring. The late sixteenth-century farmhouse and the surrounding farm buildings make an attactive scene, nestling in the hollow, when viewed across the valley road from the edge of Francis Wood.

Today's scene is somewhat less rural following the development of the Greenway estate in the fifties.

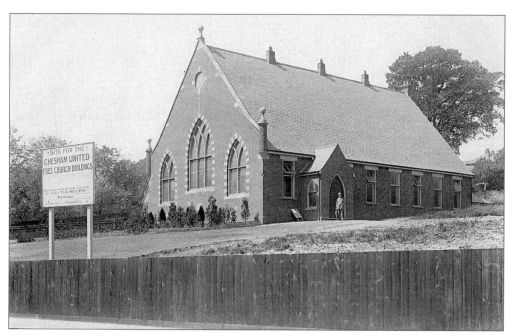

Bellingdon Road was the western limit of Newtown. Pictured here in 1907, this fine building had just been erected there for the United Free church, a breakaway from the General Baptist congregation in the Broadway.

In 1933 the church, complete with tip-up cinema seats, was sold to Chesham Methodists, who had outgrown their Broad Street chapel. They worshipped here until 1966, when this proved too small for their growing congregation, and a new enlarged church was built on the site.

Hivings Hill, the continuation of Bellingdon Road, climbs along the side of Asheridge Vale. Pictured in about 1905, building had started a few years earlier with these houses on the upper side, looking across the road and over the fields of Bottom Farm in the valley.

Part of Bottom Farm was used for allotments in the twenties, but development started there in the fifties and now covers all the fields.

This idyllic scene was the view from further up Hivings Hill, looking over the fields of Asheridge Vale in 1940. The only intrusion on the pastoral outlook was the line of houses of Berkeley Avenue, half a mile away, faintly visible on the skyline.

House-building started on the slopes of Asheridge Vale in the early sixties, and the floor of the valley has since been filled with the outsize modern buildings of an industrial estate, seen here between the houses which now line the lower side of Hivings Hill.

ACKNOWLEDGEMENTS

All the yesterday pictures are taken from postcards and photographs in my own collection.

I must express my gratitude to the original photographers, many of them anonymous, but particularly to William Butts, responsible for virtually all the pre-1900 scenes and a good many from the first decade of this century, and to William and Walter East, who produced the best photographic postcards of Chesham between the wars.

Thanks are also due to those, both visitors and townsfolk, who bought the original postcards and sent them to their friends and relations, and who eventually saved them in their own collections for their own interest, and, unknowingly, for posterity. In this connection I must mention the late King family, of Chesham and Brondesbury, who sent innumerable local cards between them in the twenties and thirties, both at home and when on holiday, and kept them until the last local member of the family died some time in the eighties.

I believe the original copyright on all the earliest pictures in this collection to have expired, but the position is uncertain with regard to those of more recent origin, and I apologize here to any copyright owners who have not been consulted. Any such omissions will be acknowledged in subsequent editions. The upper picture on page 88 is reproduced by permission of the Francis Frith Collection, Shaftesbury, Dorset SP7 8AT.

High Street from Market Square, 1905.